1st 2005 H——
Pre
And

ROAD TRANSPORT
THE READ STORY

by
Paul Heaton

P.M. Heaton Publishing
Abergavenny Monmouthshire
Great Britain
2005

Front Cover: Representatives of three haulage fleets. Richard Read's ERF ECT, VX04CDF, Harold Read's ERF ECX, X448HFU with George M. Read's MAN, WU52XAS.

Title Page: Thackwell, Longhope, where Harry and Alice Read moved in 1916.

Pages 4 & 5: Harry and Alice Read celebrate their Golden Wedding Anniversary in 1952 with their sons and daughters.
Back Row – John, Henry, George, Frederick, Ivor, Richard, Harold and David.
Front Row – Doris, Violet, Harry and Alice Read, Molly and Gladys.

All rights reserved. Except for normal review purposes, no part of this book may be reproduced or utilised in any form or by any means electrical or mechanical, including photocopying, recording or by any information storage or retrieval system, without written consent of the publisher and author.

ISBN 1 872006 18 3

© First Edition October, 2005

Published by P.M. Heaton Publishing,
Abergavenny, Monmouthshire, NP7 8NG

Printed in Great Britain by
The Amadeus Press Ltd.,
Cleckheaton, West Yorkshire, BD19 4TQ

Typeset by Highlight Type Bureau,
Bradford, West Yorkshire, BD8 7BY

CONTENTS

PREFACE

Much has been written about the transport enterprises operated from the Forest of Dean by members of the Read family, but the work has always concentrated on individual ventures, and no one has attempted to record the whole story.

I was a Police Officer in Monmouthshire for thirty years, and a motor cyclist for half that time. I remember the days before motorways and dual carriageways. The days when the roads were narrow and the heavy lorries were seriously underpowered by today's standards. The days when a driver had a puncture, and the next truck to appear stopped and help was given in changing the wheel irrespective of whether the drivers knew each other. The days when a lorry broke down on a dark night on a bend and visibility was poor and the weather bad, and the next driver stopped got his chain or rope out and towed the casualty to a straight stretch or if lucky to the safety of a lay-by. They may not have been good days, but it was a time when men, working men, helped each other.

Against that background if I came across a lorry driver travelling over the speed limit, one lucky enough to be driving a vehicle capable of doing so, three or four fingers were held aloft indicating the speed limit – thirty or forty. Headlights were flashed acknowledging the warning, and everyone was happy. You never knew when you might need that man's help in clearing the road.

Thus I knew the vehicles owned by the Reads, and whilst not knowing the driver's names, knew them nonetheless, after all they were part of the team prepared to help each other and on occasions helped me.

I got to know the fleets of George Read, Richard Read, Harold Read, George M. Read, the two-tone Green Dodge owned by Ivor Read, the bulk tipper driven by Frederick Read and met David with his ERF during the Miner's Strike. In 1997 I met Harold Read at the Bromyard Steam Rally and even sold him a book which contained a photograph of an ERF Chinese-twin which he had driven from new for his brother George.

Last year I met Frederick's son Eric, and Harold's son Philip. When I knew that they were part of the Read family I explored the possibility of compiling this book, and they were both enthusiastic. Helpfully they put me in touch with members of the family – Auntie Gladys, Uncle Ivor, Uncle Richard, Uncle (father) Harold, cousins Alan, Margaret, Donna, George, David, Adrian and Richard Jnr., who have all given freely of their time with the project.

I have started with an account of Henry Read's business following his arrival in the Forest of Dean in 1909, and thereafter accounts of the ventures founded by his eight sons. Details of enterprises started by grandsons are given, but it must be pointed out that many of the third and fourth generation are involved with the three surviving businesses – Richard Read, Harold Read and George M. Read.

I am most grateful to all those who have kindly helped with photographs and information, including Abergavenny Chronicle, Mrs. Margaret Acton, Mrs. Donna Bailey, Mrs. Gladys Barnes, The Citizen, Keith Burson, John Cox, Mark Gredzinski, Chris Morris, Dario Passaro, Mike Phillips, Adrian Read, Alan Read, David H. Read, Eric Read, George M. Read, Harold Read, Ivor Read, Mrs. Kay Read, Philip Read, Richard Read, Richard Read Jnr., Steven Read and Bob Tuck.

To anyone else who has helped – thank you. To the reader, I hope you enjoy the book as much as I have in writing it.

Paul Heaton
Abergavenny
October 2005

HENRY READ, LONGHOPE

Henry Read, better known throughout his life as Harry, was born at Hereford in 1884. He was the ninth child of John Read, a farmer, haulier and agricultural contractor, of Haywood Lodge, near Hereford, but soon after his birth his mother died. His father remarried and had a further nine children. Therefore it was no surprise that as soon as he was old enough he was expected to help his father on the farm and with his other work.

At 18 years, in 1902, he married a local girl Alice Griffiths, who was of the same age, and soon after moved to the Bristol area where he found employment using the skills and knowledge that he had learnt at home. He worked on the land and also earned a living threshing corn, using an agricultural steam engine on the drum. A year later the young couple's first child arrived – John, followed by Henry (1905), George (1907) and Violet (1908).

Harry, Alice and their four young children moved to the Forest of Dean in 1909, where initially they lived at Abenhall Mill, Mitcheldean, a house next to Wilderness Quarry. He found employment driving a steam traction engine, and by 1913 was in business on his own account with a Fowler Road Locomotive hauling timber, and subsequently cement from Mitcheldean Cement Works to Mitcheldean Road railway station, where it was transferred to railway wagons for transport further afield.

Those were the days when transport throughout the country was by rail, the only part of the journey by road being from manufacturer to the railhead, and then railhead to customer. However on one occasion he was contracted to bring heavy machinery from Gravesend in Kent to the Cement Works at Mitcheldean, the whole journey taking three weeks.

A further eight children arrived over a twenty year period – Gladys (1910), Molly (1913), Frederick (1915), Ivor (1916), Doris (1919), Richard (1925), Harold (1927) and David (1929).

His traction engine was requisitioned by the army during the First World War, and for a short period he was serving with the vehicle in France. Returning home, the family home was moved to Thackwell, Longhope, only a short distance from Mitcheldean. Thereafter he operated a steam roller, working away from home for long periods, and when possible came home on his pushbike for short breaks.

Following the war he changed direction, at first with a Foden steam wagon, and thereafter acquired his first petrol-engined lorry, an ex-War Department Peerless dropside lorry with solid tyres. Expansion followed with a second Peerless, and then a new Peerless still with solid tyres, but he soon changed the front wheels to pneumatic tyres – Michelins.

A petrol pump was installed at Thackwell and petrol was sold. The brand being ROP (Russian Oil Petrol). Expansion continued, and a Ford 6wl dropside was bought, the first in Gloucestershire, which worked well when the drive axle was in contact with the road, but a nightmare when not. Hence the subsequent introduction of the 'balance beam'.

At about this time Harry Read took a lease on Wilderness Quarry, Mitcheldean from a Mr. O.R. Roberts, who lived at Merrin House, Mitcheldean. This was a sandstone quarry, not aggregate which was in greater demand, but it nonetheless provided useful revenue.

Thereafter a Studbaker dropside was purchased followed by Leyland Cub, and a number of petrol-engined Albion KL127 dropsides. It was the days when lorries were loaded and unloaded by hand – shovel on/shovel off, the driver having a mate (usually a youngster) to assist. The tipper wasn't universally available at this time.

Most of the work consisted of coal, and the main pits served were Addis Hill at Edgehill, The Slope at Nail Bridge, True Blue at Ruardean, Eastern United at Rushbridge, Lightmoor near the Dilke Hospital, and the newer Northern United at Steam Mills. This was hauled to the Model Laundry in Session Road, Gloucester; the Hygienic Laundry in Bristol Road, Gloucester; the Stephens Jam Factory at Kingsholm, Gloucester; S.J. Moreland (the England Glory Match factory) at Bristol Road, Gloucester; and further afield to Stroud, Cheltenham and elsewhere. Timber was hauled and a number of Forest of Dean Quarries were served.

Leading up to the Second World War, construction of RAF runways created great activity and gravel and stone were in much demand in the construction. Harry's newest Albion 4wl dropside CDF279 and other vehicles were requisitioned by the military, and had to be delivered to collection centres. Son Ivor actually took the Albion to Blackwood in Monmouthshire, as instructed, by the army.

Harry continued in business until 1941, but in that year decided to retire from haulage and sold the remaining lorries to son George who was by now well established on his own account.

By this time Alice and Harry were living at Pleasant View, Church Road, Longhope, where they had a small farm, rearing pigs and chickens. They celebrated their Golden Wedding Anniversary in 1952, and a dinner was held in their honour. Amazingly it was the first time that they had their twelve children together. The first three had grown up and left home before the last three were born.

They were justly proud of the achievements of their children.

Harry Read operated this steam roller in the South West. He is seen on the vehicle.

Operating this traction engine on hauling round timber Harry Read can be seen sitting on the right on the first trailer.

The journey of this traction engine from Gravesend took three weeks. It was delivered to the Mitcheldean Cement Works.

The road under this traction engine collapsed causing it to slip over at Ruardean Hill in 1916. Harry Read can be seen crawling from under the vehicle having inspected the damage. In the background can be seen The Nelson Inn, Morse Road, Drybrook.

Opposite top left: Harry Read's second lorry was the ex-W.D. Peerless CJ4608 seen with driver Bill Brooks.

Opposite top right: Young David Read is seen with Neville 'Nipper' Williams and Richard Read who were both drivers mate's on this Albion KL127 dropside, CDG159. Note the three shovels attached to the headboard.

Left: Driver Dennis Smith and Neville Williams with the Albion CDG159.

Above: This Albion KL127 – CDF279 was requisitioned by the army leading up to the Second World War.

Right: Harry Read's Studebaker DAD687 and Albion CDF279, both dropsides in the days when they were loaded and unloaded by hand – shovel on/shovel off.

This Leyland Cub dropside was bought new by Harry Read. It is seen outside Gloucester Prison.

Above: In the late 1930s Harry Read leased Wilderness Quarry, Mitcheldean. He is seen on the left with 'Airy' Carpenter.

Below: Harry and Alice Read with their three eldest and three youngest children. at 'Thackwell'.
From the left – Henry, Harold, Alice Read, Harry Read, Richard, George, David and John.
(John and Henry were visiting from Lancashire where they now lived.)

JOHN READ & SONS, OLDHAM

John was the eldest of Harry and Alice's twelve children, and was born at Chipping Sodbury on February 10, 1903. On November 24, 1921 at Bristol he enlisted with his brother Henry in the 1st Battalion, The Gloucester Regiment (Pvte. John Read 5176509) and served for a little over three years a part of which was spent in Cologne, Germany. On January 11, 1925 he transferred to a Reservist until November 18, 1933.

He played Rugby Union for Cinderford and Gloucester where he was awarded his County Cap, and in December, 1925 signed professional for Oldham Rugby League Club, where he played for fifteen seasons.

He married at Oldham and had four children – Jack, Alan, Audrey and Ivy. Whilst John was always known in Lancashire as Jack, in Gloucestershire this was not the case – his mother wouldn't allow it.

On retiring from rugby he bought a small coal business at Oldham, together with a thirteen year old Dodge tipper which had single tyred rear wheels. To unload a loose load of slack (small coal) it had to be hand-wound to tip. Due to wartime regulations it was impossible to obtain a new vehicle.

In February, 1944, at 41 years old, he was called up and served in the Royal Army Service Corp (RASC), with the responsibility for running the business falling to his 16 year old eldest son Jack. Demobbed on February 2, 1946, he returned home to find that his son had managed to change the Dodge a few months earlier for a 3 ton Austin dropside lorry. Subsequently his younger son Alan also joined the business and a 5 ton Austin dropside was also acquired in 1948. Apart from the coal-round John and his sons also operated as carriers, and in the 1960s carried the sets for the television series 'Coronation Street' for Granada Television.

In 1959 the older Austin was replaced by an Albion Claymore 5 ton lorry with an under-slung engine and 18ft flat platform body which was supplied by his younger brother Richard from Longhope, and in 1963 another Albion Claymore arrived from Longhope.

The advent of central heating reduced the use of coal for household heating, and in consequence John retired in 1974. His son Jack carried on for a further year with the newest vehicle but then wound the business up.

John Read passed away in 1989 at 86.

Bought new in 1945 this Austin 3ton lorry CBU779 is shown in Balfour Street, Oldham, loaded with skips (baskets).

This new Austin 5ton dropside EBU755 arrived in 1948. John (left) is shown with brother Harold.

This Albion Claymore 5ton flat WDD613 shown at John Read & Sons, Cow Lane Garage, Oldham, was supplied by brother Richard as was the similar 8345AD in 1963. John Read is seen with the vehicle in the lower picture.

HENRY READ, ROCHDALE

Henry Read was two years younger than John, but joined the army with his brother in 1921. Returning to civilian life in 1925 he played Rugby Union for Lydney before moving to Torquay where he played for the local team, and married. He earned his living as a coach driver in Devon, and subsequently moved North like his brother to sign professional, but for Rochdale Hornets.

Called up, Henry also served in the RASC., and a month after 'D' –day was surprised to meet up at Arromanches with brothers John and Ivor. Whilst Henry had the cider it was younger brother Ivor who had the bottle of Scotch.

Returning home to his wife Florence after the war he resumed coach driving. They had six children – Richard, Margaret, Ivor, Geoffrey, Molly and Bernard.

Around 1950 he bought a small truck and undertook some light haulage and collected scrap. However he did not enjoy the best of health and in 1963 sadly died at the early age of 58.

Above: Henry Read seen at the wheel of this open coach when he lived in Torquay.

Opposite: Both Henry and John Read turned professional. Henry played for Rochdale Hornets RFC and John for Oldham RFC. They are seen on opposing teams at Oldham Rugby Ground at Watersheddings.

GEORGE READ, MITCHELDEAN

Hard to believe, but forty years have elapsed since the transport business founded by George Read has disappeared. Talk to any time-served haulage contractor or lorry driver in South Wales and the subject will soon turn to the days when George had upwards of thirty eight-wheelers loading out of the Ebbw Vale Steelworks of Richard Thomas & Baldwin, all on Special 'A' Licenses, all bought new, and most importantly – all paid for, and that was just part of his fleet. In these days of multi-vehicle transport operations he stood out as a pioneer and giant in the industry. It was impossible to travel from Ross-on-Wye along the A40 into South Wales towards Abergavenny without passing several of his well turned out vehicles in their maroon livery with gold sign-writing. What a sight – and all achieved by one man – shrewd, with a good business sense, prepared to invest when others feared to take the risk, and shear hard work, tinged with a little luck.

George, the third child of Harry and Alice Read, was born on March 29, 1907 whilst his parents travelled from job to job in the Bristol area, and before the family settled down for good in the Forest of Dean. At fourteen he was sent to work for his grandfather, John Read, at Haywood Lodge, Hereford, earning his board and keep and precious little else, by working on the farm, contracting to others and assisting with the operation of steam traction engines – his early taste of haulage.

After a couple of years he returned to Longhope where he worked for his father, initially as driver's mate and then driver of one of his father's expanding of lorries, operating on timber haulage, out of local quarries and transporting coal throughout Gloucestershire.

He sought to better himself, and in partnership with his father bought an ageing Dennis charabanc (open omnibus) which he converted into a flatbed lorry. Trading as H. Read & Son, his father owned half the vehicle, which was employed in hauling timber, gravel and coal in and around the area.

At this time Harry was well established at Thackwell, Longhope, and whilst George had not lived at the family home since his return from Hereford, father and son fell out. The substance of their dispute was that his father would always buy oil from salesmen who called, and supplies were of different makes and grades, whilst George believed they should be buying from one source the same grade. However George took off taking the Dennis lorry, and went to Chipping Sodbury where he hauled gravel from quarries alongside Dick Febry. Short of cash, at the end of the days work he slept in the vehicle, an uncomfortable affair, as the cab was a homemade canvas contraption.

After about a year he returned back to Longhope having earned sufficient funds to pay his father out, and their differences were mended. Thereafter he married, and set up home with his wife Elizabeth at The Firs, Plump Hill, near Mitcheldean.

He replaced the aged Dennis with a Guy and when this vehicle developed gearbox trouble he stripped it down, saw what the trouble was, and caught the bus to Gloucester to get the parts to fix it. He wisely decided that it was time to part with the vehicle, and in consequence part-exchanged it with Watts of Lydney for a new Albion diesel-engined dropside lorry.

At this time he bought a piece of land at Cookoo Patch, Mitcheldean, and obtained permission to build a house on the site. At the lower end of the plot was an old blacksmith's shop, with doors facing directly onto the road, he changed this so that the doors faced to where he was to build his home, and converted it into a workshop. At the same time he built some outbuildings for use as an office and stores, and thereafter set about building the house.

He was building the business up, buying a few old lorries which he renovated and by 1938 with war on the horizon runways were being constructed in Gloucestershire. He therefore decided to part-exchange the newer Albion in for two Bedford tippers which were employed carrying gravel and stone from the Forest of Dean for the construction.

Harry had lost some of his vehicles to the war effort, and in 1941 sold the remainder to George. Brother Frederick who had been driving for his father, continued with George for a short period until he joined the Forces.

Unable to obtain new vehicles during and immediately following the war George set about buying old Albions, which were little more than scrap, stripped them down, rebuilt them and got Nash Morgan of Whitecroft to put new bodies and cabs on them.

By this time he had bought the old Mitcheldean Transport Bus Depot at Merrin End, Mitcheldean, which was burnt out and derelict. He set about clearing the site, using the waste from Cookoo Patch to fill in and eventually had a new garage and workshop built. Expansion continued, buying ex-Army Maudslay 4wl dropsides, an Albion 6wl flat with a 6-cyl. engine, a brand new Maudslay Chinese 6 and his first ERF a brand new Chinese 6 (twin steer) six wheeler, HDF284 which brother Harold drove from new.

Around 1947 George bought Wilderness Quarry at Mitcheldean, and that year the worst weather for decades was experienced. To stop the engines freezing up, they were left running for long periods. Unfortunately no haulage work was possible for weeks and therefore no revenue was being earned. Things improved, and by this time they were involved in steel traffic out of South Wales, and the nature of their business had to an extent turned to long distance traffic.

Alas in 1949 the Labour Government implemented their policy of Nationalisation, and George's Merrin End Depot and fleet of 25 lorries fell to it. He was then appointed Branch Manager for British Road Services at Mitcheldean, at his old premises and with his old lorries. Outwardly the only change was the colour of the vehicles. One other thing different, was that he had to go to college to be taught how to run a transport fleet – the pupil instructing the teacher.

Whilst he was managing the British Road Services operation in the Forest of Dean, this meant that he could not be involved in running his own vehicles. Thus his wife Elizabeth entered the transport business, and a transport manager, Maurice Scrivens was appointed. First a brand new Albion Chieftain LAD72 was bought new from Watts of Lydney. Fitted with a Pilot tipping gear and dropside body it operated on a Contract 'A' license to a previous customer, delivering to all the old destinations throughout Gloucestershire. Being a tipper, the old shovel on/shovel off method of operation was over, and many more trips were undertaken than in the old days. It was entrusted to brother Harold.

At about the same time the local business of Roy Grindle was bought, which had three vehicles on 'B' license restricting them to 25 mile radius. One was a Morris Commercial tipper which Bill King drove at Ashchurch on the construction of a new MOD facility. Another, a long wheelbase Morris Commercial dropside driven by Sid Rivers was employed by SHACS (South Herefordshire Agricultural Cooperative Society) at Ross-on-Wye, on animal feeds, just managing to reach Avonmouth without infringing the restrictions. The third vehicle was a Bedford flatbed fitted with a detachable stock box, which was driven by George's youngest brother David. With the box fitted it served Gloucester Market two days a week hauling sheep and cattle to Ensors Abattoir at Dockham Road, Cinderford. George's son well remembers that when on holiday from school when David left the market with his first load he was left behind to sort out the next. On the other five days it was used minus the stock box on animal feeds.

During 1953 the announcement of the de-nationalisation of road transport saw George going off in his Rover 75 saloon car to visit Oxford, Gloucester, Stroud, Hereford, Newport and Pontypool to inspect the vehicles on offer, which were to be sold in groups with their Special 'A' licenses, the various Lots being tendered for. His old depot at Merrin End had been expanded considerably during the last four years, with in addition to the 25 licenses of George Read's original fleet the vehicles of Cornwall of Mitcheldean and others had been added. He tendered for numerous groups of vehicles throughout the region, and also tendered for his old Merrin End depot with all its vehicles. The hope was that he would be successful in some of the offers.

George's son recalls going downstairs one day at home before setting out for school, and seeing his father pacing up and down the kitchen with a look of sheer joy on his face having just opened his mail, and declaring, "I've got the jackpot". Indeed he had. His tender offers had been successful in securing his Merrin End premises together with in excess of 100 vehicles. Well over a 100. He hadn't exactly expected this result but with the support of his bankers took the lot.

What happened next was a nightmare. As he took delivery of the vehicles it was discovered that many had been sabotaged by the BRS drivers. Sugar in fuel tanks, sand in engine sumps, and much worse. Fitter Jim Russell, George's main man on maintenance had much to do to put all this damage right, but it was achieved. As a result when BRS asked George if he would take the drivers on, he said, "Tell them to come and see me for a job". He interviewed every man himself.

The majority of the vehicles acquired were Albion Chieftain and Albion Clydesdale 4 wheelers, and clearly he never had need of so many. Other hauliers had not tendered – being put off by the numbers, or had put in unrealistic offers. Thereafter he sold off individual lorries with licenses, many only wanting single vehicles. Having bought in bulk, he now sold off many of the vehicles at considerable profit.

Having made so much money, he set about using some of these funds to uprate the fleet before the taxman took it. He had never owned an eight wheeler, but in the next few years was to buy around thirty – Leyland Octopus and AEC Mammoth Majors' fitted with coil wells. Much of his work was steel out of Ebbw Vale and later Llanwern. But good management saw the vehicles laden in both directions.

A contract with Richard Thomas & Baldwin at Ebbw Vale required that large amounts of tinplate were stored and brought forward for distribution when required. As a result George had two warehouses built at Mitcheldean for this purpose.

A surplus of coal in the Forest of Dean saw him investing in tippers, running to Uskmouth Power Station near Newport. Other work saw coal and coke being hauled out of South Wales. He had a contract to carry a load per day of lump coal from Royal Arms Colliery, Dowlais to Paddington Hospital, and acquired an AEC 8wl bulk tipper for the job. It was before the motorway network, thus the vehicle was run 24 hours a day. Empty from Mitcheldean to Dowlais, loaded back to Mitcheldean. Change drivers load delivered in London and back empty to Mitcheldean. The vehicle was fitted with a 5 speed gearbox, and when George discovered that his son had ordered a 6 speed box to replace it, he raged "you'll ruin me" and "it'll just give the driver an extra hour in the cafe". Although he never admitted the wisdom of this move, it is interesting that more 6 speed gearboxes appeared in the fleet.

Brother Richard had gone into articulated vehicles in 1957 when he bought his first. George was more cautious, but in 1962 he did start to acquire some.

Sadly George died in 1962. He had fought cancer for fifteen years, a fact not known by many outside the family. It is difficult to believe that he was only 55 years old when he passed, having achieved so much.

His widow Elizabeth, son George and daughter Ann had to contend with the burden of death duties, and as joint shareholders often had to buy secondhand vehicles thereafter, but they carried on with the business, ably assisted by Maurice Scrivens, who was as loyal to them as he had been to George before.

Mrs. Read had read that the British Road Services were being allowed to buy good transport businesses, and as a result contact was made, the vehicles and Merrin End premises inspected, and a meeting was arranged, and a price agreed. Thus in the Summer of 1965 the George Read fleet passed back for a second time into the hands of BRS. A condition of the sale was that George's son should not be involved in road transport for a period of ten years on his own account. But like his father before, he became Branch Manager at Merrin End.

Above: Initially George Read went into partnership with his father trading as H. Read & Son. George, left, is seen with the timber feller Leonard Bowkett.

Opposite top: Alice Read with son George's first new lorry, an Albion KL127 dropside delivered by Watts of Lydney.
Right: These rebuilt Albion KL127 dropside lorries were normally employed on transporting coal from the Forest of Dean to laundries in Gloucestershire. This example – BOM916, dates from before the Second World War.

George and Elizabeth Read with their children George M. and Ann in the Second World War.

This ERF 6wl (Chinese Twin) dropside, HDD284 arrived in the George Read fleet new in 1948 and was allocated to brother Harold to drive.

*Haulage
Contractors*

*General Goods
Any Distance*

GEORGE READ

(G. & E. A. READ)

MITCHELDEAN, Glos

BRITISH ROAD SERVICES
(Road Transport Executive)
UNIT No. G. 47.

Merrin End Garage,
MITCHELDEAN, GLOS.

Dear Sir/Madam,

We beg to advise you that in accordance with the Transport Act, 1947, this business will be acquired by the British Transport Commission on the 11th May, 1949, and will from that date be carried on under the title Road Transport Executive Unit G.47.

I shall continue, as Manager of this Unit, to deal with your requirements in the usual way.

May I take this opportunity of thanking you for your past business and co-operation. I trust you will continue to give your support to the undertaking in the future, which I assure will continue to serve you well.

Yours faithfully,
p.p. GEORGE READ,

Dear Sir/Madam,

We have to advise you that, as and from the 11th May, 1949, the Road Transport business hitherto carried on by Messrs. George Read, (Proprietors G. & E. A. Read), Mitcheldean, Glos, has been acquired by the British Transport Commission and will be operated by the Road Transport Executive, on their behalf, under the title shown at the head of this letter.

We can assure you of the same good service as has been provided in the past and we trust that the good relationship which has existed will be continued.

Yours faithfully,

Divisional Manager,
Western Division,
Road Transport Executive.

Opposite top: Letters sent to customers from George Read and the Divisional Manager of British Road Services informing them that the business was being Nationalised on 11th May, 1949. George Read's was the only 'Read' business to fall to the 1947 Transport Act.

Opposite bottom and right: This Albion 4wl dropside tipper LAD72 was operated by George's wife Elizabeth transporting coal to many of the old customers in Gloucestershire. Bought new from Watts of Lydney, George, being the British Road Services Manager at Mitcheldean was unable to declare an interest. The vehicle was driven by brother Harold. Harold's wife Mary and Harry Read are shown in the photograph on the left.

Above: This 1953 Leyland Comet dropside was the first new vehicle bought following denationalisation in 1953. Previously the business had operated as a partnership but in that year it was incorporated as George Read (Transport) Ltd.

Two views of part of George Read's fleet of Albion dropsides at the Merrin End Garage in 1955.

In the years immediately following de-nationalisation George Read was to buy new in excess of thirty eight-wheelers. This AEC Mammoth Major MK.3 was the first, and it was put in the charge of brother Harold.

The first of the initial order of Leyland Octopus 8wl flats to arrive in the fleet was PDF605.

Leyland 8 wheeler RAD668 laden with tinplate from Ebbw Vale.

The dimensions and weight of this excavator shovel raised a few eyebrows when it arrived at Mitcheldean as a return load back into South Wales.

The Merrin End Garage with six AECs and six Albions in view.

Eight Leyland and nine AEC 8 wheelers can be seen in this view with eight Albions at Mitcheldean.

Five 8wl flats laden with cable drums from Lydbrook.

Driver Roy Duggan is seen with this AEC Mammoth Major 8wl flat TDF672 at the Jungle Cafe, Shap. In the background can be seen Leyland Octopus 8 wheeler, 1103AD.

Some idea of the size of the George Read fleet can be seen in this view at Merrin End in 1957. The Leyland Octopus 8 wheelers were numbered: PDF605, PDF606, RAD667, RAD668, RDG515, SAD228, SDD963 & TAD235.

Opposite top: There are several of these long-wheelbase Leyland Comet tippers in the fleet. YAD100 was normally used on coal and coke traffic.

Opposite bottom: Five LAD-cabbed Leyland Comets seen with a batch of Leyland 8 wheelers.

Above: AEC 8 wheeler and drawbar trailer TDF670 laden with bagged apples for delivery to H.P. Bulmer Ltd., Hereford.

Overleaf: An impressive view of six Leyland Octopus 8 wheelers, consecutively numbered. 1100AD-1105AD.

The new AEC Mammoth Major Mk.5 1394AD seen on the outside lifting ramp.

This view shows that by the early 1960s the fleet was being continuously uprated with modern vehicles, mostly from AEC.

This view of Merrin End shows a group of ten AEC 8 wheelers. The vehicle to the left of the pump is a bulk tipper which carried a load of lump coal daily from Dowlais to Paddington Hospital, London. The five vehicles on the right consist of AEC 6wl Mustang and Marshall models, including at least one bulk tipper.

This AEC Mammoth Major Mk.5 8-wheeler 2559DD arrived new in 1961.

Another well turned out unit of the George Read fleet is this AEC Marshall 6wl long-wheelbase tipper 6037DD.

Workshop Staff at the Merrin End Garage.

Back row: Chris Meek, fitter; Jim Richards, Motor electrician; Derek Austin, driver; John Dibell, foreman; Joe Jones, fitter; George M. Read; Ernie Matthews, fitter; Dennis Dickinson, fitter; Geoff Johns fitter; Michael Burns, fitter.

Front row: Howard Roberts, wash down; Mike Turley, forklift driver; Stan Thomas, fitter; David Workman, battery boy; John Hyett, driver; Derek Burns, wash down; Joe Gregory, wash down.

This AEC Mercury articulated outfit ADG611B is seen having just loaded steel coils at the Ebbw Vale Works of Richard Thomas & Baldwin, Articulated vehicles started to appear in the fleet in the early 1960s.

I can't think of many fleets which had the signwriters lining on the trailer as well as the tractor unit.

AEC Mandator articulated outfit 9823DF dated from 1963.

AEC Mercury ADF611B at Ebbw Vale Works before the load has been sheeted.

FREDERICK READ, ROSS-ON-WYE

Frederick Read, born in 1915, when he left school at fourteen was sent to work for his grandfather John Read at Haywood Farm, Haywood Lodge, Hereford. He didn't like farming and after a year or so returned back to Longhope where he worked as a driver's mate for his father. Usually carrying coal from pits in the Forest of Dean and railway wagons at Parkend Railway sidings mainly to laundries in Gloucester, Cheltenham and Stroud. When he was 16 he went on to drive for his father still carrying out the same work – shovel on/shovel off, and three loads carried per day. In the Second World War, when his father retired from haulage and his lorries passed to his elder brother George, he went to work for him until he joined the army. He was always regarded as the 'Top Driver' no man could load a lorry with coal faster.

Returning from the armed services in 1946 he spent a year or so back driving for George, and then set out in business on his own account with an Albion 4wl flat lorry operating on a restricted 'B' carrier's license which allowed him to transport agricultural produce over any distance, effectively exempting him from nationalisation. He operated carrying hay and straw mostly into South Wales.

Living at Ross-on-Wye, he married, and they had two children Eric and Clive. In the early 1950s he had exchanged the Albion for a Leyland Comet 4wl dropside, uprated the license and obtained work with the Hereford firm of H & G Thynne, carrying their products, usually tiled grates/fire places to all parts of the country. This meant that he was away from home for up to three days at a time carrying out up to nine drops.

Eventually he found further work at Whitehead Steel at Newport, and the Ebbw Vale Steelworks of Richard Thomas & Baldwin. His fleet was increased to three vehicles including a Dodge 6wl flat, an Albion Reiver 6wl flat and a Seddon 8wl flat fitted with a Gardner 150 engine. Both these latter vehicles were supplied by Praills at Hereford, and all were fitted with a coil well, and finished in his green livery.

Constant delays waiting to load at Ebbw Vale brought him to the decision to sell up, and the vehicles passed to Matthews Bros., of Hereford. Thereafter he spent three or four years buying and selling army surplus and other products, but in 1968 he re-entered haulage when he bought a Dodge 4wl tipper which he used hauling gravel and stone from quarries in the Forest of Dean. Around 1972 he changed this vehicle for an Albion Reiver 6wl bulk tipper and hauled coal and coke out of South Wales to the London area, and scrap back into Wales. In 1980 at 65 years he retired from haulage and became a warehouseman for a tool business at Ross-on-Wye. Finally retiring in 1985 at 70 years of age.

His son Eric has driven for a living all his adult life, and for a period operated a Ford D1000 articulated bulk tipper fitted with a Perkins V8 engine, whilst his brother Clive is a painter and decorator.

Fred's quiet personality endeared him to many, and his connections when needed often found employment for his brother's lorries. He died in 2003 at 88 years of age.

This Leyland Comet 4wl dropside GCJ169 was employed carrying tiled fire grates for H. & G. Thynne of Hereford.

Above: Fred Read is seen with his Leyland Comet GCJ169.

Opposite top: This Seddon 8wl flat 298ACJ and Albion Reiver 6wl Flat XCJ72 together with a Dodge 6-wheeler were operated out of Richard Thomas & Baldwin's Ebbw Vale steelworks.

Opposite bottom: Fred Read with his younger brothers at a function c2000. From left – Harold, Richard, Fred and Ivor.

IVOR READ, LONGHOPE

Born on September 17, 1916, Ivor Read on leaving school at 14 joined the army – the 1st Battalion Royal Berkshire Regiment (8.8.1931) and on Christmas Eve of that year set sail for India in the troopship Dorsetshire. Celebrating Christmas Day in the Bay of Biscay he was amazed to be treated to a meal of 'spuds with jackets on'. He served in India, thence the Sudan returning to England in 1935.

He left the army in 1937 and thereafter worked for his father, passing his driving test in 1938 on the new Albion 4wl dropside CDF279. Carrying out the full range of jobs for his father he was saddened when this vehicle was requisitioned by the army, but thereafter drove a Leyland Cub.

His age for call up came, so he volunteered and joined the Royal Army Service Corp, and served in Northern Ireland, Normandy, through France, Holland, Belgium and Germany.

He left the army in 1947 and went to work for brother George and opened the new garage at Merrin End. George had a big fleet of Albion KL127 4 wheelers, and at first he converted a number of these from petrol to 4LK diesel engines. After a few years he left and set up on his own repairing cars, electrical installations and lighting plants. After a while he went into timber haulage a very skillful job, and hauled a lot of timber in its full length, which would not be allowed today. Employed on this work he had a number of Thornycroft Nubian tractor units with pole carrying trailers, an FWD Su-Coe timber tractor and Bedford QLs, all being ex-WD.

He found that the reward for this work was never up to its volume, but also had a Dodge articulated tractor unit with a 4 in line bulk tipper trailer which he operated on coal and coke out of South Wales. Fitted with a Perkins 6.354 engine and operating at 24 tons gross, he described it as a donkey doing the work of a horse.

In 1968 he sold up, and thereafter went to work for his brother Richard where he spent 27 years. He lives in Longhope with his wife happily in retirement.

Opposite: Having joined the army at 14, Ivor Read sailed for India on December 24, 1931, on the troopship Dorsetshire. He returned to Southampton on the same ship from Port Sudan in 1935.

Top: In the early 1950s Ivor Read entered business as a timber haulier, often operating these ex-WD Thornycroft Nubian timber tractors.

Above: A site is cleared.

This Thornycroft Nubian tractor and pole trailer LAD16 were hauling timber in long poles from Cefn Mably to Rhiwderin Sawmill.

This page and overleaf: Driver Len Turner lost control of this vehicle at Cinderford. Fortunately nobody was injured.

This ex-WD FWD Su-Coe timber tractor GUE655 was used by Ivor Read.

This Thornycroft Nubian HDF286 has tipped on its side into a reen.

Ivor Read used this Dodge articulated bulk tipper carrying coal and coke out of South Wales.

RICHARD READ, LONGHOPE

Visit the Forest of Dean today and you would be unable to miss the contribution made to the local economy by Richard Read and his family. The businesses he has founded are major employers in the area. The origins of Richard Read (Transport) Ltd go back 58 years and now operate a considerable fleet of ERF articulated vehicles at 44 tonnes maximum gross vehicle weight throughout the United Kingdom and Europe, from its base at Longhope. Computerised warehouses are maintained at Cinderford and Longhope where customer's products are securely stored and brought forward for distribution as required. Richard Read (Commercials) Ltd was incorporated in 1960 with a close association being forged with ERF who appointed the firm as their distributor for Gloucestershire, Herefordshire and Worcestershire, and today this is maintained with MAN-ERF. Offering a full service from sales, service, repairs and recovery. The whole operation runs 24 hours a day, seven days a week.

Richard the tenth child of Harry and Alice Read was born at Longhope on November 6, 1925, and on leaving school he was to be found working for his father as driver's mate on one of his Albion KL127 dropside lorries delivering coal around Gloucestershire, in the days before tippers, when it was shovel on/shovel off. At sixteen he was driving one of his father's vehicles. In the war Harry Read passed the remnants of his fleet to son George, and at this time Richard enlisted in the Royal Navy.

Returning to Longhope in 1946, initially he worked for brother George, but later in that year he married Amelia and set out on his own, sinking wells by hand in order to build up a stake to enable him to enter road haulage on his own account. This was hard work, and after a year he used the £350 he had saved up to buy an ex-WD petrol-engined Albion 6 wheeler. Gloucester Ring Road was being constructed and he found work carrying stone to the site from a quarry in the Forest of Dean. He recalled hauling 625 tons in his first month in business. 625 tons shovelled on / 625 tons shovelled off. Thereafter he obtained a contract to haul 30,000 tons of stone for Severn Water Authority, but saw the wisdom of converting the Albion into a tipper with the gear from an old Morris Commercial.

Thereafter a 4wl Dodge tipper was bought, and when the Albion wore out he replaced it with a new Bedford 'O' type 4 wheeler. Expansion continued and by 1949 seven vehicles were being operated. Whilst Richard was still driving, Amelia ran things from home – effectively carrying out the role of transport manager.

Because of the localised nature of his work he avoided nationalisation, but was thereafter restricted to operating within a 25 mile radius. Any further distance was only covered if a permit could be obtained. There was a way around this, however, but he had to know who he was dealing with and trust them. Own account vehicles operating on a 'C' licence were exempt from any kind of restrictions. Thus he would actually buy the product, transport it, and then sell it to the customer, invoices taking account of the product value plus haulage costs.

Originally based at his cottage home at Little London, the vehicles were parked on a farm at Royal Spring. However as he expanded he moved to Pleasant View, Church Road, Longhope, where his parents had retired to, and where he and Amelia built a bungalow – "Greystones", and brought up their children – Sheila, Brenda, Richard and twins Alison and Ian.

Brother George, eighteen years his senior, had following the nationalisation of his fleet been the Branch Manager for British Road Services at Merrin End, Mitcheldean. With the denationalisation of transport he had made offers, for various lots of BRS vehicles being offered for sale by tender, including the Merrin End garage. George was successful in obtaining far more vehicles than he actually wanted and set about selling some together with their all important Special 'A' licenses. Richard knew this. He also knew that George had set the price he wanted, and brother or no brother, he wouldn't be swayed. So Richard went to see George, expressed an interest in nine vehicles being offered and within hours agreed to buy them.

Interestingly George had not even taken delivery of the vehicles and Richard agreed to fetch them himself. Legend has it that a few were actually at the Mendalgief Road Works of Whitehead Iron & Steel Co. Ltd., at Newport, Monmouthshire, and when he and his drivers arrived to collect them, he was asked if he wanted loads to go on them. What an offer. Forty years on he was still sending lorries back there. Interestingly, George Read's main customer in South Wales was Ebbw Vale Steelworks. No Richard Read vehicle loaded there, and no George Read vehicle loaded at Whiteheads'. Whilst the Read brothers might compete with others, they certainly wouldn't compete against each other, after all blood is thicker than water!

An important customer of Richard Read was the tile manufacturer H & G Thynne at Hereford and he had a number of vehicles on this work. In 1955 he bought his first eight-wheeler, an Atkinson dropside with Gardner engine, David Brown Gearbox and Kirkstall double drive bogie.

The local nature of much of his earlier work had given way to more and more long distance traffic, and in consequence the size of individual vehicles was increasing.

In 1957 he was visited by Harold Sansum, Sales Manager for ERF who convinced him to buy his first vehicle from this manufacturer. Mr. Sansum had a hard job, but convinced Richard that his favoured specification might actually be better in an ERF. Coincidentally this first ERF was to be the first articulated vehicle in the fleet.

Having outgrown their Church Road base, it was no surprise when he acquired a site on the edge of the village, which was far more suitable for the expanding operation. By coincidence it was very near Thackwell, where his father had operated from between the wars. The move took effect in 1957.

All was going well, too well. The sudden collapse of Thynnes' at Hereford, a major customer, created a heavy dent in the business. Not only had they lost the work, but he lost money on haulage already carried out.

At the time he had three eight-wheelers on order with ERF and contacted the manufacturer to say that he could now only afford the one.

Those at Sun Works had a good feeling about Richard Read, telling him to pay for the other two when he was able to. This helpful gesture was much appreciated by Richard and Amelia, and when 13 months later they had settled for the two vehicles Richard asked how much interest was due for the deferred payment, Dennis Foden's response was "Keep on buying ERFs, that's all we would like".

Expansion continued. Much work was undertaken out of Whiteheads' at Newport and The Sudbrook Paper Mills became an important customer. Bulk tipper work was being undertaken with coal and coke out of South Wales, and deliveries of coke to schools and other outlets was carried out. In fact a wide range of customers was being served.

The association with ERF was sealed when Richard Read was asked to become their distributor in Gloucestershire and Herefordshire (and later Worcestershire), and Richard Read (Commercials) Ltd was formed in 1960 for this purpose. The original haulage business was incorporated on March 21, 1963 as Richard Read (Transport) Ltd.

In the 1960s the fleet had risen to an all time high of 87 vehicles, all under the day-to-day control of Amelia, an amazing feat for the mother of five children. It cannot be over emphasised the key role she undertook in the development of the business.

In 1974 Richard Read joined in a £7 million contract transporting agricultural equipment to Baghdad (Iraq) which was to last two years. Vijore was formed with Eric Vick and Tony Jones, the name being a compilation from Vick, Jones and Read. At the end Richard withdrew leaving continued involvement in the hands of Vick and Jones. He was unhappy with the changing pattern of seeking groupage which he thought made it harder to organise and control.

In the late 1970s Richard Read suffered a driver's strike in furtherance of a pay claim. He felt that the demands were unreasonable, and would not yield. Who could have over eighty vehicles standing idle, not earning any revenue? The only answer was to dispose of some of them. Indeed he auctioned off over three-quarters of his fleet, survived, and raised very good prices by the sale.

Prior to the Miner's Strike of 1984/85 he had a dozen bulk tippers, rigid and articulated outfits hauling coke out of Port Talbot Steelworks to Commonwealth Smelting at Avonmouth. His nephew George Read was also involved in this traffic, and during the strike the vehicles were subjected to a great deal of attention. Vehicles were smashed up, drivers threatened, and even after meetings with the striker's representatives they stated they had no intention of stopping their actions.

The Reads decided to carry on, whilst others had parked up their vehicles, and as a result made application at the High Court in London for an injunction to prevent this abuse of their staff and vehicles. On April 11, 1984 Judge Sir Douglas Frank, QC granted the injunction under the provisions of the Employment Protection Act against the South Wales Area of the National Union of Mineworkers. The actions of the NUM continued and on July 31, 1984 the Reads went back to court and, for failing to comply with the injunction the NUM was fined a total of £50,000. In the case of the Avonmouth traffic from Port Talbot vehicles left Port Talbot independently every five minutes or so, with the Police keeping a watchful eye on their progress.

One of the most significant events during this strike was the supply of iron ore, coal and coke to the Llanwern plant of the British Steel Corporation. This had always been carried by rail from Port Talbot where BSC had their own deepwater terminal where giant bulk carriers landed cargoes of iron ore and coal, for use at Port Talbot itself and also for onward transmission to the Llanwern plant. When the rail union stopped their members from crossing picket lines, effectively stopping supplies reaching Llanwern, this threatened production and indeed the long-term future of the works. Convoys of bulk tippers with vehicles from a wide range of operators were set up in order to supply the works. These convoys ran under Police escort. There was an iron ore convoy of over a hundred vehicles and a coal and coke convoy of about 50 vehicles running twice a day. In the morning whilst the iron ore convoy left Port Talbot laden, the unladen coal/coke convoy was leaving Llanwern in the opposite direction. On arrival at Port Talbot the vehicles were loaded, whilst the ore vehicles were tipping at Llanwern, and so on. This operated for almost a year, vehicles were damaged and protective mesh grills had to be fitted to windscreens in an effort to protect driver's from flying missiles.

Richard Read employed around six vehicles on this traffic whilst his nephew George M. Read had several so employed. Richard's brother David and his son David H. Read, both owner drivers had their vehicles on this job too.

Eventually the strike ended, picketing ended, but it was to be a long time before this traffic returned to the railway. Thereafter the vehicles carried on but operating on their own blending in with the normal traffic.

Gradually over the past two decades the nature of Richard Read's haulage business has changed taking account of differing work coinciding with a contraction in South Wales' industries which has seen a significant reduction in the traditional steel, coal and coke traffic.

Richard Read (Transport) Ltd branched into warehousing in 1976, building a 30,000 sq.ft warehouse on it's Longhope site. A second 16,000 sq.ft warehouse followed later.

In 1995 the company acquired a site at Cinderford and established the major part of it's warehousing operation there, with two warehouses of 74,500 sq.ft and 21,500 sq.ft, together with office accommodation. However, the 'hub' of the business continues to be at Longhope.

Over the years it has also expanded it's Heavy Recovery business, building up an impressive fleet of recovery vehicles under the care of Richard Read Jr. Richard fully admits that there is nothing quite like getting a lorry 'back on it's wheels' and nothing will keep him away from the challenge! Richard and his family attend the various Truckfest shows around the country, during the year, and if requested participate in recovery demonstrations in the arena.

Various members of Richard and Amelia's family have worked in the business over the years. Richard Jr. the eldest son joined in 1977 and Brenda their daughter in 1971. Richard and Brenda are today Directors of the company and take an active role in the running of the business.

Richard's wife, Kay, has also worked in the family business since 1979 and their eldest son, also Richard (b.1985) is now in the final year of his HGV mechanic apprenticeship. Second son Christopher (b.1988) is preparing for his GCSEs and youngest son Simon (b. 1992) is very keen to join his father working in the recovery side of the business, as soon as possible.

Richard and Amelia's eldest daughter Sheila and her husband Royston have two sons – Paul worked for some time in the warehouse but now has his own building firm and Martin, who worked in the parts department, then vehicle sales; transferring to MAN ERF UK Ltd when ERF was taken over and the sales team taken on by them to sell to the customer direct.

Richard and Amelia's youngest son Ian, worked in the business many times over the years, as an HGV driver and in the warehouse. Sadly Ian lost a long battle with ill health and passed away last year. Ian's twin sister, Alison, too worked in the business for many years but decided to move into a new career a couple of years ago. Ian's eldest son, Mark (b.1983) has recently moved to the village and started work in the warehouse at Longhope.

Richard and Amelia's nephew, George M. Read's son – Edward, joined the company in 1994 and was recently promoted to General Manager of the MAN ERF side of the business.

Mrs. Amelia Read stated, "Both Richard and I never imagined, when we started in business all those years ago, that the company would have grown to the size that it is. The most pleasing part, is that we have met so many people over the years, many of whom have become our personal friends. My family have been involved all along and this also gives me great pleasure".

This Dodge tipper FAX450 was Richard Read's second vehicle. It normally hauled out of Forest of Dean quarries.

Left: Richard Read with his first new vehicle, a Bedford 'O' type, KFH8 seen at 'Greystones', Church Road, Longhope.

Opposite top: This Thornycroft 4-wheeler NAE565 was not a success in service, often suffering from engine problems.

Opposite bottom: This Maudslay Mogul 3 dropside HWO238 dating from 1950 was one of nine vehicles bought from brother George. It had originally been a British Road Services vehicle based at Pontypool.

Below left: An Albion KL127, GXE866 is seen with two Bedford QLs at 'Greystones'.

Opposite top: This Atkinson 8wl dropside arrived new from Praills of Hereford on June 1, 1955. It was Richard Read's first eight-wheeler, and is photographed at 'Greystones', Church Road, Longhope. Seen from the left are Jim Cowmeadow, Amelia Read, Richard Read and Margaret Dobbs.

Opposite bottom: The Gardner 6LW engined Atkinson 8 wheeler MVJ681 was still in the Richard Read fleet ten years later.

Above: This Bedford 'S' type dropside TAD698 was employed carrying tiled fire grates for H. & G. Thynne of Hereford. The vehicle's load could involve up to nine drops and was often away for as long as three days.

Above: This Albion 6wl flat RDD223 is loaded with steel from Whiteheads' at Newport. I don't know what Atkinsons thought of the badging.

Left: Another Albion 6wl flat, SAD590.

Richard Read's first ERF. This ERF KV articulated tractor until TDF689 arrived in the fleet in 1957 and was powered by a Gardner 6LW engine. Its acquisition coincided with the move to new premises at the edge of the village.

A series of ERF 8 wheelers based on the KV chassis were bought new from the manufacturer. ERF 8wl drawbar outfit UDF307 is seen delivering a navvy grab to Barry Docks which called for the tyre pressures to be reduced to negotiate a bridge. Driver Harold Waite has his back to camera, and trailer mate Owen Price is nearest trailer.

This ERF 8wl flat fitted with a Gardner 6LW engine is seen leaving London enroute to Machen Paint Works in South Wales with drums of resin.

This Dodge long-wheelbase tipper RDF34 is loaded with flint destined for the tile manufacturer H. & G. Thynne, Hereford.

Richard Read seen clearing the forecourt at the new premises.

With a backdrop of ERF KV vehicles – Richard and Amelia Read with their three children – Sheila, Brenda and Richard Jnr. Twins Alison and Ian hadn't arrived yet.

This ERF 8wl flat was fitted with a Gardner 6LX (150) engine.

In 1960 Richard Read (Commercials) Ltd. was incorporated and the firm was appointed as the ERF distributor for Gloucestershire, Herefordshire and Worcestershire. An early customer was Richard's cousin Tracy in Hereford who bought this ERF KV 6LW engined tractor until RVJ70.

Driven by John Cox this Dodge tractor unit with 4-in-line trailer is seen in Western Avenue, London, carrying drums of resin destined for Machen Paint Works.

Richard Read's Dodge tipper 3977AD being loaded with excavated materials at Harold Read's. Richard Read was also distributor for Dodge vehicles.

Driven by John Cox this ERF 3978AD was the first articulated tractor unit to be fitted with the Gardner 150 (6LX) engine.

Richard Read (Commercials) Ltd. had a stand at the 1963 Three Counties Show at Malvern. Mrs. Amelia Read is shown with the ERF tractor unit supplied to cousins – T. J. Read & Sons. Fitted wiht a Gardner 6LX engine it was registered 758DCJ.

The 1964 stand of Richard Read (Commercials) Ltd. at the Three Counties Show at Malvern.

Seen at the Three Counties Show this ERF 8wl rigid was fitted with bodywork by Atkinsons of Clitheroe which enabled it to self-discharge.

This ERF was one of a number of vehicles delivering coal and coke to hospitals and schools.

Four ERF LV vehicles, both tractor unit and 8 wheelers at Longhope. From the left PDF239G Noel Morris, TDG421H Eddie Overthrow, TDG422H Ray Emery and TDG423H Ron Lewis.

This Cummins-engined ERF tractor unit and bulk tipping trailer MAD561F operated out of South Wales on coal and coke, and was driven from new by brother Harold.

This ERF tractor unit PDD707G was engaged on general haulage.

ERF Chinese-twin 6x2 tractor unit PDF239G was fitted with a Rolls Royce 220 engine and 10 speed Fuller box. It is loaded with steel from the Whitehead Iron & Steel Co. Ltd., Mendalgief Road, Newport.

This ERF 8wl bulk tipper TDG421H fitted with a Gardner 180 (6LXB) engine, operated with coke out of South Wales.

The left hand drive ERF tractor unit NFH120P was used on Continental work.

Fitted with a Gardner 240 (8LXB) engine this steel-cabbed ERF tractor unit HDF228N was used on the Middle East contract.

From 1974 Richard Read joined in a contract transporting agricultural equipment to Baghdad. Vijore was formed with Eric Vick and Tony Jones, the name being a compilation from Vick, Jones and Read.

Whilst this contract involved Iraqi traffic, calling for part of the journey through Germany being on the railway, it was to extend even further afield. Destinations included Turkey, Syria, Jordan, Iran, Saudi Arabia, Qatar and even one journey into Pakistan. Apart from Baghdad, journeys were undertaken to the south of Iraq at Bandar-e Shaphur and Bandar-e Abbas. The vehicle was extremely well equipped and all manner of spare parts were carried. Return loads were arranged by agents – dates from Iraq being a common cargo. Most favoured were spools for nylon back to Gloucestershire.

Two ERFs waiting in Germany to be loaded onto the railway for the journey into Yugoslavia.

Richard Read in the desert.

ODG666M crossing the desert.

Keith Burson at the wheel of NFH251P, powered by a Cummins 335 engine.

Convoys of bulk tippers were employed during the 1984/85 Miner's Strike transporting coal, coke and iron ore from Port Talbot to British Steel Corporation at Llanwern. A Richard Read ERF articulated bulk tipper passes along the M4 Motorway in convoy at the Coldra.

A line of fifty bulk tippers about to leave Llanwern Steelworks empty for Port Talbot. An ERF 'B' Series is seen on the left.

This ERF 'B' Series tractor unit SDD364R is fitted with protective mesh.

"Private enterprise is defending itself! What bad taste—it should be nationalised!"

Cartoon which appeared in the Daily Express – August 1, 1984.

This ERF 8wl bulk tipper SAD562W fitted with gready boards was used to transport coke out of South Wales.

This ERF 'B' Series UYF547S was a rare purchase from other owners.

Richard Read had an important contract transporting foundry coke from Port Talbot steelworks to Commonwealth Smelting at Avonmouth. ERF 8wl tipper SYX998S would have been employed on this work.

Supplied new to other owners, when LAW971P was taken in part exchange it was converted into a tipper for coal and coke traffic. It is seen on the outside of a 'C' Series ERF 8wl tipper YDD963Y.

This 'B' Series ERF 4x2 tractor unit TJS922W is operated with a tri-axle bulk tipper trailer. Richard Read operated out of many of South Wales' pits and coke ovens and whilst ever increasing size vehicles entered the fleet, access difficulties at delivery point sometimes dictated that 8 wheel rigids continued to be used.

This ERF 'C' Series tractor unit TFH988X dated from 1982.

Another unit of the bulk tipper fleet is this ERF – B716BFM.

ERF 'C' Series 6x2 tractor unit A201KDG with tri-axle bulk tipper trailer.

ERF – A201KDG with steel coils.

John Cox loading ERF 'C' Series B286ODF at Mon, Belgium.

A trio of demountable buildings being transported by units of the Richard Read fleet, led by ERF B716BFM.

B286ODF having just loaded newsprint at Sheerness Docks. This vehicle was fitted with a Cummins 290 engine.

ERF 'C' Series tractor unit AUD52Y forming part of the general haulage fleet.

ERF 'C' Series tractor unit C30SFH with bulk tipper trailer.

A new ERF 'E' Series C924XDD.

This 1987 ERF E14 tractor unit D256FDD forms part of the bulk tipper fleet.

Twenty ERF tractor units in this line-up at Richard Read (Transport) Ltd., Longhope.

Three ERF E14 tractor units – J2RRT, J4RRT and G241EAD.

The main part of the Richard Read (Transport) Ltd. warehousing operation is at purpose built premises at Cinderford.

This curtainsider semi-trailer displays the product of a customer. The tractor unit is an ERF EC11 – R485JFH.

Another view of the Cinderford Warehouse Complex. Another product is advertised.

This ERF EC11 outfit R485JFH displays the product of a customer.

100

Opposite top: This ERF ECX 6x2 tractor unit VX51HGP forms part of the present Richard Read fleet.

Opposite bottom: Richard Read Jnr. with son Simon in front of the modern ERF ECT tractor unit VU52XEG.

Above: MAN tractor unit WX54FZV with ERF ECT – VX03AAF.

Right: This ERF ECT tractor unit VX04CDF forms the prototype for a Corgi model in 2005.

Opposite top left: MAN box van X338FRE whose bodywork is in the livery of UK Pallets.

Opposite top right: ERF EC6 4w1 curtainsider.

Opposite bottom: MAN 4w1 curtainsider WX54GBV in the livery of UK Pallets – Express Delivery.

Above: This ERF KV 6 wheeler was acquired and restored by Richard Read.

Above: John Cox who retired in 2003 after 48 years service with Richard Read. There are a number of long serving employees – Miriam Knight is currently the longest serving, having completed 41 years.

Scammell Pioneer recovery vehicle once operated by Richard Read (Commercials) Ltd.

Built originally as a heavy duty tractor until for export this vehicle was bought new. Changes to Trade Plate legislation meant that it was later registered as Q399FDD. It has recently been completely rebuilt in its current form.

6x4 ERF recovery vehicle GFH884V seen approaching Monmouth from Ross-on-Wye in December, 1994.

E524GRK seen at Truckfest South in July, 1998.

ERF EC12 tractor unit with lowloader trailer allows for the complete recovery of long vehicles particularly coaches which due to their construction do not lend themselves to being suspended.

Modern lowloader outfit based on an ERF ECX 6x4 tractor unit VE02VOC.

Rigid 6wl recovery vehicle again for complete lift, based on an ERF EC12 chassis. It is fitted with a slide bed.

Units of the Richard Read recovery fleet seen at a recent Truckfest.

This MAN 6x4 recovery vehicle 550TGX entered service in 2005.

HAROLD READ, LONGHOPE

Harold Read was born at Longhope on August 24, 1927. On reaching fourteen, when he left school he was sent to learn farming at a farm in the shadow of Dinmore Hill, near Ludlow. He hated it, and after six months returned home. At this time his 26 year old brother Ivor was home on a short leave from the army, and that was it. The very next day, still only fifteen he went to the Recruiting Office at Brunswick Road, Gloucester, and signed up. Of course he was too young, but declared himself as 17. As he jubilantly left the office, the recruiting sergeant shouted after him, "How old are you?" To which he replied, "Seventeen, Sir", to which the sergeant replied "Good boy, don't forget".

He was allocated to the 1st Battalion of the Buckingham Regiment, and sent to Ayr Racecourse in Scotland for training. Whilst there he celebrated his sixteenth birthday, and was that age when he landed at Normandy on 'D' Day. Harry and Alice Read had six sons and a daughter in the armed forces during the war – an anxious time. They needn't have worried as all returned unscathed. Harold being the last to return, came home in 1947, and still only 20.

He immediately went to work for brother George, and a year later was entrusted with his brother's pride and joy, a brand new ERF 6wl (Chinese twin) dropside lorry, index number HDF284. This vehicle was transporting steel out of Richard Thomas & Baldwin, Ebbw Vale, and when George's business was nationalised, he continued to drive it.

Alas, all was not well, as soon as it was realised in Ebbw Vale Works that he wasn't a member of a trade union, they refused to load him. He was still only 21 but wouldn't join – feeling that having served his country in war, he wasn't going to be dictated to. Brother George, now manager of the Mitcheldean depot of British Road Services was powerless to intervene, and Harold was sent to see District Manager – Mr. T.S. (Tommy) Thomas at Lydney. Whilst he received every sympathy and was treated with respect, the result was that he and the BRS parted company.

Whilst George was with the British Road Services, he still had Wilderness Quarry, and Harold was set to work for his brother in the quarry, driving a 10RB excavator. When a new Albion 4wl dropside tipper was bought new in George's wife Elizabeth's name he was put in charge. Thereafter he transported coal around Gloucestershire and was actually serving many of the customers that his father had in the 1930s.

George had been successful in getting back his Merrin End depot from British Road Services in 1953 in the de-nationalisation scheme and had secured in excess of a hundred vehicles all with licenses. Having made a substantial profit in the sale of some of these, he was investing in a fleet of brand new 8-wheelers, and the first an AEC Mammoth Major was entrusted to Harold.

Not surprisingly Harold wanted to go into business for himself, and encouraged by his wife Mary, he bought a Leyland Comet 4wl dropside off his brother. Thus on November 15, 1954 at 27 he became the proud owner driver of his first vehicle. Early work consisted of coal being delivered around Gloucestershire for his brother, but he was soon hauling out of Ebbw Vale, where the Transport Manager remembered him. Being the owner of the vehicle he could hardly be a union member, and they were pleased to give him work.

At first he operated out of his brother's Merrin End Garage in Mitcheldean, but as he expanded he secured premises in Church Road, Longhope. The Leyland Comet was sold to H.L. Robinson at Hereford, and replaced with an Albion Chieftain 6 wheeler. Thereafter he operated three vehicles, Dodge 4 and 6 wheelers, and in 1960 bought a brand new ERF 8 wheeler off brother Richard. In 1964 he had another ERF 8 wheeler followed a year later by an ERF articulated outfit with tandem axled coil trailer. All were hauling steel out of Ebbw Vale, and back-loading into Wales with whatever was on offer. Much of the steel traffic was to the North-East, and returning loaded was important.

Eventually the profitability of his business was affected by the long delays experienced at Ebbw Vale where the works was now trading as the British Steel Corporation. On occasions a vehicle was waiting up to 30 hours to load, and he felt that this just could not go on. In 1967 the decision was taken to sell up, and his modern fleet of three ERFs sold to Richard, for whom he then worked, at first driving, but later as night fitter.

He and Mary had four sons, Philip, who was serving his time at the Gloucester depot of Watts of Lydney, Adrian (whose twin Nicholas sadly did not survive) and Mark. After three years with Richard, Harold decided to start up on his own again. In 1970 he bought an Atkinson 8 wheel bulk tipper from his nephew George M. Read and set about hauling coal and coke out of South Wales, sometimes animal feedstuffs, but usually scrap back into South Wales.

Whilst Harold was operating an 8 wheel bulk tipper he was always convinced that the way forward was with maximum weight articulated outfits, and when he became aware that an Atkinson tractor unit was lying at Sharpness without an engine he bought it. In his spare time and with help from Philip he set about rebuilding this vehicle. The best thing about the 8 wheeler he was using was its engine and when the work was almost complete on the tractor unit he and his son transferred it over. A bulk tipper trailer was bought and he was operating at maximum weight.

In 1973 Philip left Watts' and went to work for his father. They operated the Atkinson outfit night and day. Coal and coke out of South Wales and scrap back. However in 1974 the Miner's strike reduced the work and whilst enough could be found to run the vehicle normally, there was no way that they could now run it 24 hours a day. Philip then went to work for Uncle Richard.

For the next five years Harold remained an owner/driver, replacing the Atkinson in 1976 with an ERF. Mick Russell who lived locally had been trying to persuade Harold to buy another vehicle so that he could go and work for him. In 1979 he bought a second outfit and took Mick on – and he has been with him ever since. Later the same year he bought a third vehicle and son Adrian joined him.

The work usually consisted of coal and sometimes coke out of South Wales and whatever could be found to haul back into Wales – usually scrap, some coal from opencast in the Forest of Dean and in the summer a bit of stone. The fleet was gradually expanded and more drivers taken on. After a while it was found that the coal work wasn't operating efficiently. A vehicle capable of carrying 19 tons was leaving loaded with 14 or so tons, and they were unable to get the extra put on. As they only got paid for the weight actually carried this affected the profitability of the business. There was a shortage of vehicles on scrap, and as a result he took on more of this work.

His son Philip had been in business on his own account since 1976, and was operating bulk powder tankers on cement, a bulk 8 wheeler and an ERF articulated tractor unit with a bulk trailer. In 1993 Philip sold the 8 wheelers and joined his father and brother Adrian in the partnership, incorporating his articulated outfit in the Harold Read fleet.

They have operated over a dozen tractor units with twice as many trailers in their red and maroon livery. Scrap, the main part of their business now, is very hard on the trailers, and much work is undertaken to keep them in tip-top condition. Harold and his sons pride themselves on their modern well presented fleet.

Whilst Harold has two sons in the business, a third generation has been working in the garage for ten years – Philip's son Steven.

Harold and Mary still live in Church Road, Longhope next to the garage and yard – it could hardly be said that he has retired.

Harold Read bought this Leyland Comet 4 wheeler MDD316 from his brother George thereby setting out on his career as a haulage contractor on his own account.

Harold Read bought this Albion 6wl flatbed TDF673 and is seen here with it laden with cable drums from the Siemens-Ediswan factory at Lydbrook.

This Dodge 6wl flat is laden with steel sheet from Richard Thomas & Baldwin's Ebbw Vale Steelworks.

Opposite: Harold and Mary Read with sons Philip and Adrian with the ERF 8wl flat 2442AD which arrived new in 1960 – his first new vehicle.

Top: Harold Read with his ERF KV 8wl flat 2442AD.

Above: In 1964 a second ERF 8wl flat AAD619B was bought from brother Richard.

Another view of the new ERF KV 8 wheeler showing bodywork with coil well by Nash & Morgan, of Whitecroft. This vehicle was normally operated out of Richard Thomas & Baldwin's, Spencer Works, Llanwern.

Harold Read's fleet in 1965. ERF LV articulated tractor unit with Highway tandem axle coil trailer EDF555C powered by Gardner 150 (6LX) engine, and ERF KV 8 wheelers 2442AD and AAD619B fitted with Gardner 150 (6LX) engine.

Top left: Having worked for his brother Richard for three years in 1970 Harold went back into business when he bought this Atkinson 8wl bulk tipper HJS30 from his nephew George M. Read. He has operated bulk tippers ever since.

Top right: Subsequently he replaced the 8 wheeler with this Atkinson tractor unit and bulk tipper trailer, 708DWN.

Above left: 708DWN loading at a quarry in the Forest of Dean.

Above right: Harold and Mary Read's youngest son Mark at Church Road, Longhope. Tragically Mark was fatally injured whilst pursuing his hobby of Schoolboy Motor Cycle Scrambling.

This 1976 ERF 'B' Series tractor unit NHS674P and bulk tipper trailer loading at Wilderness Quarry, Mitcheldean.

This ERF 'B' Series 6x4 tractor unit SUH396S is seen loaded with scrap at the Longhope premises.

ERF tractor unit DMS692S at the garage at Longhope.

These three vehicles have just loaded foundry coke at Port Talbot Steelworks. ERF 'B' Series SUH396S, ERF 'C' Series A77JAD and Philip Read's ERF 'B' Series WDF286S which was subsequently absorbed into the Harold Read fleet.

This ERF 'A' Series tractor unit NDF987M was bought from Eric Vick Transport. Originally intended for use as a shunter, it was in such good condition that it was used in the main fleet for a few years.

ERF – NDF987M tipping scrap at Alpha Steel, Corporation Road, Newport.

ERF 'A', 'B' and 'C' Series tractor units of the Harold Read fleet.

ERF 6x2 – A77JAD has just completed loading scrap and is ready to leave.

ERF articulated outfit A77JAD loading at Swansea docks.

This ERF 6x2 'C' Series A90WBO was bought from Nestle at Chepstow. It is seen at Whitchurch, Ross-on-Wye in April, 1995. It is still used as a shunter.

Above: This ERF 'A' Series tractor unit GHG656N was used as a shunter at Gloucester.

Below: This well turned out shunter for on site work was an ERF LV – BLM504H.

Another view of the 6x2 ERF A77JAD at Longhope.

This 6x4 ERF 'C' Series C27SFH is seen at Malpas Road, Newport in October, 1992.

Opposite top: Mick Russell is seen with ERF – C27SFH. When he left school in 1958 he worked for George Read as a trailer mate, and subsequently worked for George M. Read. He has been with Harold Read now since 1979.

Opposite bottom: ERFs A112CSX and C27SFH.

Above: An impressive view of ERF 6x4 tractor unit C27SFH at Longhope.

Opposite top: Two units of the Harold Read fleet unloading scrap at Tremorfa Steelworks, Cardiff. ERF 6x2 – B203CHB and ERF 6x4 – C27SFH.

Opposite bottom: The ERF 'C' Series B203CHB tipping its load of scrap at Tremorfa Steelworks, Cardiff.

Above: This ERF 6x4 outfit C538VBF is seen travelling along the motorway.

Overleaf: The old lining from the incinerator chimney of the Glourcester Royal Hospital is loaded onto a step-frame trailer drawn by this ERF 'C' Series tractor unit C759AVF.

Opposite top: ERF 6x4 tractor unit E666YMB at Longhope, a unit of the present fleet.

Opposite bottom: ERF 'E' Series 6x2 articulated outfit F735AUH.

Top: Another ERF 'E' Series tractor unit D94NAX.

Above: Yard scene at Longhope showing the twelve vehicle fleet of Harold Read.

This ERF 'E' Series – J3RRT was bought from brother Richard.

ERF – J4RRT is seen loading at European Metal Recycling at Gloucester.

Above: R441UDD is one of a pair of consecutively numbered ERF EC11 tractor units. The other being R440UDD.

Below: Another ERF EC11 is T921ASO.

Harold Read's ERF ECX tractor unit and tri-axle bulk tipper trailer X446HFU being loaded with steelwork during the demolition of the Gloucester Megabowl on May 7, 2004. (The Citizen).

Opposite top: ERF ECS 6x2 tractor unit X976MKM with tri-axle bulk tipper trailer at the Church Road Garage, Longhope.

Opposite bottom: Mick Russell with ERF ECX – Y975RDF at Avonmouth Docks.

Above: Harold Read shown with his ERF ECX – Y975RDF at Longhope. The vehicle operating at 44 tonnes GVW is fitted with a Cummins 440 engine.

ERF ECS tractor unit VX03ACJ with new tri-axle bulk tipper trailer. Built by Rothdean's of Cinderford who supply all Harold Read's trailers.

Two modern units of the Harold Read's fleet, both ERF ECS – WX53ATY and VX03ACJ.

Three of the fleet at an ERF REVS Show: ECX -- Y975RDF, ECS – VX03ACJ and EC11 – R440UDD.

Part of the fleet at Hereford Truck Show – 2004.

ERF ECS tractor unit VX03 ACJ which was supplied new by brother Richard.

DAVID A. READ, TAYNTON

David Alan Read who was born at Longhope on November 24, 1929 was the twelfth and last child of Harry and Alice Read. When he was born some of his brothers and sisters had already left home, and indeed the eldest John who was almost 27 already had children of his own.

When he left school he followed in the footsteps of some of his brothers being sent to Haywood Lodge, Hereford where he was put in the charge of his grandfather John Read. Here he was introduced to farming, but it is interesting to note that whilst so many of the Read brothers shared this experience none was so impressed that they took it up as their future livelihood.

Thereafter he was called up and following National Service returned to Gloucestershire where he went to work for his brother George, or more correctly George's wife Elizabeth. He drove a Bedford cattle truck out of Gloucester market for two days a week, and at other times with the livestock box removed was usually employed carrying fertilizers around local farms.

When George took over the Merrin End depot back from British Road Services he continued driving for him for a while but spent much of his employment thereafter as a fitter in and around the Forest of Dean.

Around 1970 he decided to go into business on his own account, and bought a Bristol articulated tractor unit and bulk tipper trailer from his nephew George M. Read. This vehicle was employed hauling coal and coke out of South Wales and whatever was on offer back into Wales. Having operated this vehicle for a while he bought an Atkinson tractor unit off George to replace it. Whilst still operating as a driver/owner he successively owned another Gardner 6LXB engined Atkinson and an 8LXB engined ERF.

In 1980 he bought a brand new ERF 4x2 tractor unit from his brother Richard. This vehicle powered by a Cummins 290 engine was operated out of South Wales usually with coke and nephew George undertook the job of finding the work for him in the early days.

In the 1984/85 Miner's Strike he was to be found hauling coal and coke out of Port Talbot steelworks bound in convoy to British Steel Corporation's Llanwern plant, also out of Orb Works, Newport where materials were being landed on their river wharf and transported by road into Llanwern, and independently with coke out of Port Talbot bound for Commonwealth Smelting at Avonmouth.

Thereafter the usual pattern of trade resumed and he continued as a driver owner until the late 1980s when ill-health resulted in his early retirement. Sadly in 1992 he died at 62, being survived by his wife and six children – Jennifer, Elizabeth, Gillian, Carol, David Harry and Rachel.

Opposite left: David Alan Read in the Forces.

Opposite right: Bristol tractor unit 268BCY which David Read bought off his nephew George M. Read. To the rear is the Atkinson which he replaced it with. Also shown are Philip Read, Harold and David.

Top left: Harold with his sons Philip and Adrian with the Atkinson tractor unit they had rebuilt for David.

Top right: Another view of the Atkinson David bought off George.

Above left: David with Atkinson TTG429G.

Above right: David operated this ERF 'B' Series tractor unit fitted with a Gardner 240 (8LXB) engine.

Above: David Read travelling in his ERF 'B' Series GAD170V along the M4 Motorway Eastbound at the Coldra. During the 1984/85 Miner's Strike convoys of lorries supplied iron ore, coal and coke to Llanwern Steelworks from Port Talbot. His vehicle is carrying coal on this job.

Left: David Read bought this ERF tractor unit GAD170V from brother Richard. It was fitted with a Cummins 290 engine.

GEORGE M. READ, MITCHELDEAN

George Merry Read was born on June 29, 1939, the son of George and Elizabeth. He had an incredible grounding in road transport in his childhood and youth, and vividly recalls many of the events surrounding the operation of his father's business. The post-war expansion, nationalisation, British Road Services, de-nationalisation, further expansion, articulation, culminating in the sad death of his father on October 22, 1962. All this and George was still only 23 years old.

It might be imagined that as an only son he would have been spoilt. None of this – his father expected him to pull his weight – and this he did. One story highlights this – one dark wet and windy night a driver had been taken ill at Ebbw Vale works. He was sent to get the vehicle, still barely 21, he arrived to find the eight wheeler and drawbar trailer ready loaded and sheeted, the trailer man being little more than a boy himself. Setting out from the works he undertook the long climb from the works across to Beaufort through Brynmawr, and started the long steep and narrow descent of the Blackrock. Crawling down the rock, would have been bad enough in daylight on a fine day, but at night in bad weather it was a heart stopping experience. The arrival on the flat down towards Abergavenny being met with considerable relief.

Following the death of his father, the business was carried on for a further 2$^1/_2$ years much to the good offices of Transport Manager Maurice Scrivens. With the sale to British Road Services in the Summer of 1965 George became Branch Manager at Merrin End, a position he was to hold for about twelve months.

Although restricted from entering road transport for a period of ten years, the family still owned Wilderness Quarry at Mitcheldean. Thus young George, now 27, started up on his own with plant hire, excavation and demolition work. He built up the plant and a fleet of tippers for this work.

With the ten year restriction soon to expire he had the opportunity of putting some vehicles on contract, hauling coal and coke again out of South Wales and scrap metal back into Wales, and eventually built up a fleet of fifteen bulk tippers – 8 wheelers and articulated outfits.

During the 1980s Miner's Strike he had vehicles in the coal and coke convoys operating under Police escort from Port Talbot to Llanwern, and had other vehicles running from Port Talbot to Avonmouth, and took part with his Uncle Richard in applying for an injunction against the NUM to prohibit the abuse to drivers and damage to vehicles.

In 1988 the bulk tipper fleet was sold, and he concentrated on the skip hire/waste disposal, waste transfer business. The demand for sandstone in house construction has increased, in consequence the quarry work has expanded.

Currently over a 100 skips are in use, three skip lorries, a Foden 38 ton gross tractor unit with ejector trailer, and two 8 wheel ERF tippers which take away dirt and waste from the quarry.

George has four children – Jane is a teacher in Kent, Nigel who was a fitter and driver for his father is now sales manager with Gunn JCB at Hereford, Edward is general manager with Richard Read (Commercials) Ltd whilst Jonathan works at Wilderness Quarry.

George has been an elected District Councillor for Mitcheldean for 34 years and is the present Chairman of the Forest of Dean District Council, and has been a Parish Councillor for 31 years. In 1984 he was awarded the MBE.

Left: This Dodge tipper was the first vehicle to enter George M. Read's fleet in 1966. It was operated from Wilderness Quarry, Mitcheldean.

Overleaf: This Atkinson tractor unit UEA676G arrived in George M. Read's fleet in 1970.
Note that it was fitted with a sleeping pod.

Opposite top: This Leyland Super Comet skip loader SFH300G is shown next to an Atkinson.

Opposite bottom: This Dodge 4w1 dropside tipper VSO950S was used to deliver supplies of stone from Wilderness Quarry.

Above: This Atkinson tractor unit DDF830L formed part of George M. Read's bulk tipper fleet. Coal and coke was hauled out of pits and coke ovens and from the Phurnacite plant at Mountain Ash to all parts of the country, and scrap was normally hauled back into Wales.

Above: Cummins-engined ERF 'B' Series YVL372S.

Below: This Gardner 240 (8LXB) engined Atkinson LAD755P was fitted with a sleeper pod.

Above: Due to access delivery problems at some locations there was a need for 8 wheelers. This ERF with Gardner 180 engine YVH682R is fitted with greedy boards.

Below: Both these vehicles were bought new – ERF LAD755P and Atkinson LDD784V.

Opposite top: During the 1984/85 Miner's Strike convoys of tippers were employed carrying supplies of coal, coke and iron ore from Port Talbot to British Steel Corporation at Llanwern. In this view an Atkinson of George M. Read's is seen travelling along the M4 Motorway at Coldra. The vehicle is laden with coal.

Opposite bottom: The second vehicle in this view is an ERF owned by George M. Read seen on the M4 Motorway Eastbound near Cardiff.

Above: Part of George M. Read's fleet of bulk tippers seen at Wilderness Quarry, Mitcheldean. Note that they are all of ERF and Atkinson manufacture.

Richard Read (Commercials) Ltd. holding an ERF Promotion at Ross-on-Wye. The 'B' Series tractor unit on the right is displayed prior to delivery to nephew George M. Read.

Here and opposite: This ERF EEA300T is seen delivering stone from Wilderness Quarry to Goldcliffe.

159

ERF – EEA300T delivering stone to the river bank at Brecon.

EEA300T travelling from Ross-on-Wye towards Monmouth in September, 1994.

Looking down from Wilderness Quarry, Mitcheldean.

The scene that met Welsh Office Minister Gwillym Jones and Roger Evans, M.P. for Monmouth as they arrived to attend a site meeting at Llanellen Bridge, on the main A4042 Abergavenny to Pontypool Road in 1995.

The ERF 8wl tipper TFE525W managed to pass after a short delay. Local residents were overjoyed that this happened infront of their elected representatives as they were campaigning for the construction of a footbridge. To date, 2005, nothing has been built.

This MAN skip lorry WU52XAS is part of George M. Read's present fleet.

PHILIP H. READ, LONGHOPE

Born in 1951, Philip is the eldest of Harold and Mary's four sons. On leaving school he took an apprenticeship as a commercial vehicle fitter with Watts of Lydney at their Gloucester facility, and having obtained his City & Guilds remained for a further two years with Watts'. It was a good background for what was to come.

In 1973 he went to work for his father, and they operated an Atkinson articulated bulk tipper outfit 24 hours a day, hauling coal and coke out of South Wales. The 1974 Miner's strike reduced the available work, and whilst Harold carried on as a driver owner, Philip went to work for Uncle Richard, at first as a fitter at his Longhope garage, and later a driver.

In 1976 he bought his father's Atkinson and set out in business on his own account. Thereafter he bought and sold another Atkinson and then an ERF LV tractor unit was bought. In 1978 he bought a brand new 'B' series ERF tractor unit from Uncle Richard. This was a 4x2, and was fitted with a Cummins 290 engine. He operated this with a bulk trailer on coal, coke and scrap, and for a period of about a year operated out of Llanwern Steelworks with a coil trailer. In 1984 he bought a new tri-axle bulk tipper trailer, and continued as a driver owner.

Whilst continuing to operate the ERF bulk tipper outfit, in 1987 he took the opportunity to expand when he bought an ERF bulk powder tanker from Rugby Cement. This was a 6 wheeler which he used hauling powdered bulk cement from Rugby Cement's Gloucester Depot to South Wales and the South West. He also on occasion hauled from Rugby or Southam depot to the silos at Gloucester. A year later he sold this vehicle and replaced it with an 8wl ERF powder tanker which was used on the same work. Over the next year or so he acquired a further three tankers, one of which was used carrying flour. Eventually one of the tankers was converted to a bulk tipper. At one stage Philip was operating a total of five ERF vehicles.

The bulk cement work started to dry up, when an increasing number of owner drivers were employed, thus from 1992 Philip, in stages started to dispose of the vehicles. In 1993 he had disposed of the last 8 wheeler and then entered into partnership with his father and brother Adrian, bringing his ERF articulated outfit with him which was incorporated into the Harold Read fleet.

Philip has two sons, Steven who served his time at Richard Read (Commercials) Ltd at Longhope and later worked for British Road Services at Gloucester, and Michael who also worked in the garage at Richard Read. Since 1994 Steven has worked at Longhope in the business founded by his grandfather.

Philip Read started up in business in 1976 when he bought this Atkinson tractor unit 708DWN from his father.

He subsequently owned this Atkinson LTX903E. Shown are Philip Read, son Steven, father Harold and friend John Williams.

This ERF – WAE640H was owned by Philip Read for a short time.

This ERF 'B' Series tractor unit WDF286S was bought new from Uncle Richard in 1978. It is seen loaded with lime from Redland Quarry at Taffs Well.

ERF WDF286S is seen travelling from the direction of Ross-on-Wye towards Monmouth in September, 1994.

Philip Read bought this ERF 6wl powder tanker BHP507T in 1987 and employed it on hauling cement in bulk from Rugby Cement at Gloucester.

This 'B' Series ERF 8wl powder tanker HDU910V was also employed in transporting cement.

This ERF – HDU910V is seen discharging cement at Cheltenham.

Phil Read's powder tankers HDU910V and EBF916T loading at Rugby Cement's silos at Newport.

ERF 8wl powder tanker EBF916T discharging cement at the Redland Quarry, Taffs Well.

Four units of Phil Read's fleet: ERF articulated bulk tipper WDF286S, ERF 8wl powder tanker EBF916T, ERF 8wl powder tanker HDU910V and ERF 8wl bulk tipper TFE525W.

Phil Read's ERF tractor unit WDF286S and new tri-axle bulk tipper trailer being loaded at Gloucester.

WDF286S loading scrap during the demolition of Oakdale Colliery in Gwent.

Phil Read's ERF WDF286S and his father's ERF C27SFH unloading at Liverpool. The top of the load is being removed by grab before the vehicle can tip.

DAVID H. READ, CINDERFORD

David Harry Read was born on November 24, 1959 sharing a birthday with his father David. He was an only son, having five sisters. When he left school he spent a period working on local farms, and when he was seventeen worked in the workshops of Rossiter & James, Hauliers of Parkend.

In 1981 he entered into business when he bought an ERF 8wl bulk tipper, fitted with a Gardner 6LXB (180) engine. The vehicle was employed on the usual trade out of South Wales with coal and coke, with scrap backloaded, cousin George finding the work. The lorry although being owned by him was operated on the Operator's License of his father. For a period of eight months he used a Volvo F86 with a bulk tipper trailer, whilst he rebuilt the ERF, but thereafter resumed work with the 8 wheeler.

Like his father he was employed carrying coal and coke from Port Talbot to Llanwern during the Miner's Strike of 1984/85 and at other times hauling coke out of Port Talbot, a vehicle leaving every five minutes destined for Avonmouth. Later during the strike he was operating in the North of England.

Around 1986 he sold up and drove for someone else for a while, and in the late 1980s worked in the workshops of Uncle Richard at Longhope. In 1990 he set out on his own with workshops at Lydney undertaking work for a number of Forest of Dean hauliers.

Whilst in business at Lydney, he has lived throughout at Cinderford, with his wife and two children.

He has a particular interest in commercial vehicle preservation and has completely restored a 1958 Morris Commercial 4wl flat.

Above: David Read is working on his ERF 8wl tipper with father and friends looking on.

Below: David H. Read with his Volvo F86 tractor unit.

Overleaf: David H. Read has restored this 1958 Morris Commercial 4750E to as new condition.

P.M. HEATON PUBLISHING

Paul Heaton was born at New Inn, Pontypool, in 1944 and was educated at Greenlawn Junior School in New Inn and the Wern Secondary School at Sebastopol. At fifteen he commenced employment, at first in a local store and then with a builder's merchant. A year later he was appointed as a Deck Cadet in the Merchant Navy, with the Lamport & Holt Line of Liverpool, and served in their vessels Chatham, Constable and Romney usually in the Brazil and River Plate trades. He joined the Monmouthshire Constabulary (now Gwent) in 1963, and served at Abergavenny, Cwmbran, Newport, the Traffic Department, the Motor Cycle Section, as the Press Liaison Officer, and for five years represented Inspectors for the whole of Wales nationally on the Joint Central Committee of the Police Federation. He was promoted to sergeant in 1974 and Inspector in 1982. On his retirement he served as Market Inspector with the RSPCA for eight years and at the same time was Landlord of a Public House for three years. He has always maintained an interest in maritime history and in transport generally, and has had the following books published:

Reardon Smith 1905-1980 (1980)
The Baron Glanely of St. Fagans and W.J. Tatem Ltd., with H.S. Appleyard (1980)
The 'Redbrook', A Deep-Sea Tramp (1981) four editions
The 'Usk' Ships (1982) two editions
The Abbey Line (1983)
Kaye, Son & Co. Ltd., with K. O'Donoghue (1983)
Reardon Smith Line (1984) two editions
The South American Saint Line (1985)
Welsh Blockade Runners in the Spanish Civil War (1985)
Lamport & Holt (1986) two editions
Tatems of Cardiff (1987)
Booth Line (1987)
Jack Billmeir, Merchant Shipowner (1989)
Welsh Shipping, Forgotten Fleets (1989)
The Gallant Ship 'Stephen Hopkins' with R.J. Witt (1990)
Palm Line, with Laurence Dunn (1994)
Not All Coppers Are...! (1994)
Wynns – The First 100 Years for John Wynn (1995) three editions
Wynns – The Last 20 Years for John Wynn (1996)
L.C. Lewis, Heavy Haulage (1996)
Wynns Overseas first draft for John Wynn (1998)
The Wynns Fleet – 120 Years of Road Haulage (2003)
Lamport & Holt Line (2004)
Road Transport Gwent (2004)
Road Transport – The Read Story (2005)
Road Transport Monmouthshire (2005)
Road Transport Wales & Border (2005)